Foraging for Beginners

Edible Herbs and Plants All Year Round

Disclaimer: All photos used in this book, including the cover photo were made available under a Attribution-ShareAlike 2.0 Generic (CC BY-SA 2.0)

and sourced from Flickr

Copyright 2016 by Publisher - All rights reserved.

This document is geared towards providing exact and reliable information in regards to the topic and issue covered. The publication is sold with the idea that the publisher is not required to render accounting, officially permitted, or otherwise, qualified services. If advice is necessary, legal or professional, a practiced individual in the profession should be ordered.

- From a Declaration of Principles which was accepted and approved equally by a Committee of the American Bar Association and a Committee of Publishers and Associations.

In no way is it legal to reproduce, duplicate, or transmit any part of this document in either electronic means or in printed format. Recording of this publication is strictly prohibited and any storage of this document is not allowed unless with written permission from the publisher. All rights reserved.

The information provided herein is stated to be truthful and consistent, in that any liability, in terms of inattention or otherwise, by any usage or abuse of any policies, processes, or directions contained within is the solitary and utter responsibility of the recipient reader. Under no circumstances will any legal responsibility or blame be held against the publisher for any reparation, damages, or monetary loss due to the information herein, either directly or indirectly.

Respective authors own all copyrights not held by the publisher.

The information herein is offered for informational purposes solely, and is universal as so. The presentation of the information is without contract or any type of guarantee assurance.

The trademarks that are used are without any consent, and the publication of the trademark is without permission or backing by the trademark owner. All trademarks and brands within this book are for clarifying purposes only and are the owned by the owners themselves, not affiliated with this document.

Table of Contents

Introduction 5

Chapter 1 – Prep 6
   Bad Veggies 6
   Prepping 8

Chapter 2 – Easily Identifiable Plants 11
   Onions 11
   Chives 12
   North American Dandelion 13
   Cattails or Reeds 13
   Purple Clover 14
   Shamrocks or Wood Sorrel 15
   Wild Carrots 15
   Orange Daylily 16
   Curly Dock 16
   Violet 16
   Garlic Mustard 17

Chapter 3 – Poisonously Edible Plants 18
   North American Thistles 18
   North American Nettles 18
   Blackberries 19
   Wild Cherries 19
   Milkweed 20
   Acorns 20

Chapter 4 – Medicinal Plants 21
   Broadleaf Plantain 21
   Weeping Willow Bark 21

    Pine Tree Leaves 22
    Red Sumac 22
    Mayapple 23
    GoldenRod 23
    JewelWeed 24

Conclusion 25

FREE Bonus Reminder 26

Introduction

Welcome to Edible Plants and Herbs To Forage All Year Round, a book focused on the northern parts of the world to provide you with a collection of foods that grow during different times of the year. This book can be used as a gardening tool or a as needed survival guide for immediate foods in your area as one can always bolster their survival rate with more knowledge about their surroundings. Let's begin.

Chapter 1 – Prep

A lot of flora is good for you, but you need to realize that some flora is poisonous and some flora is just plain bad for you. Actually, let's go over what it means to be "bad" for you because a lot of people don't realize that not all veggies are good for you and some of them are not even veggies.

Bad Veggies

This is something that some people have difficulty wrapping their head around, but, odds are, these individuals are like-minded to those who think that meat is made in a market rather than grown on a farm. It requires a bit more inquisitive thought to an otherwise pointless topic for most.

First off is that you should avoid eating the seeds of all the wild food because seeds are bad for you. The only way to fix a "bad" seed is to let it sprout, which is to say that you should let it grow before you eat it if you plan to eat it unroasted. This is because seeds have a layer of chemicals that prevent you from retaining or absorbing vitamins such as calcium.

Secondly, most stems are also bad for you unless the plant itself is the stem because most stems have the most dietary fiber in them. In our daily lives, dietary fiber isn't a bad thing and we do need a small portion in our daily meals to get a well-balanced diet. The problem arise when eating a few stems and you're suddenly over 300 percent of what you need. This means that nearly all of the nutrients you bothered trying to eat will now be shoved out the backend instead of being absorbed because the body tries to get rid of dietary fiber once it realizes that you can't digest it. This is why dietary fiber is considered a laxative and why too much of it can actually kill you.

Thirdly, try to stay away from veggies that are obvious foods as in you know that even a child could recognize it as a food like a carrot. While these are easy to spot, this also means they're easy to spot if you are a wild animal or bug. Therefore, if you take a bite of one of these you might find that you're getting some added protein from a couple ants or even roaches. The problem lies in the fact that insects will tend to bury themselves into the core of the veggie because it is a good place to eat while also not having to worry about predators because the predator can't x-ray the veggie. Some extra protein might not be so bad, but if you get a bug with a poisonous skin then you're likely to have some problems.

Prepping

Although you may try to stay away from obvious veggies, those might be the only ones around you so you need to know how to properly prepare all veggies to make sure they're relatively safe to eat. Unless you have access to a lab, you can't be one hundred percent confident that the food you're about to eat is going to kill you but you can certainly make sure that you are relatively confident.

The first order of business is to make sure you take a twig and push aside the branches on the food to make sure you're not going to get bit when you grab the food. This is common with items such as bananas, which have the banana spider that will hide among the root to catch any unfortunate insect that things the banana is going to be their food for the next couple of days. A banana spider can kill you very quickly, so ensure you know how to inspect for little predators on plants is a good first step in making sure your food won't kill you. The reason why the banana spider will still bite you even though it recognizes you are too big to be food is that it is a defensive measure to kill you first before you have a chance to kill it.

The second order of business is to make sure there aren't any holes inside of the veggie. You can do this by feel, which can be unreliable, or you can do this by water. When you do this by water, you just have to pour water on it and see if the water bounces anywhere. This will signify that there is just something that cause the water to go off of the veggie or inside a hole, fill up, and then force water out of the veggie.

Once you have done that, it's now time to **KILL IT WITH FIRE** but not really. Essentially, you need to boil it until it is safe enough to eat. Stick it in a pot of filtered water and bring it to bubbling. Once the water is bubbling, it is actually past the point where it needs to kill all the different pathogens on it. This is needed because even though animals may not have eaten it, that doesn't mean that nasty bacteria haven't crawled all over the plant you want to eat. In order to get rid of it you have to boil it, which is why the most commonly collected plants are plants that are good for a nice stew or for flavoring meat.

Listen to this, you need to not try to sustain your body on only veggies. Many survivalists have died trying to do this because society makes them believe being a vegetarian is good for their body. It is good for your body in a sedentary life, but not an active one. They try to carry their meatless diet into the forest only to find that they quickly die of starvation due to the lack of fat mixed with how many calories you burn when you try to survive in the wild.

If you cannot identify what the plant is right off the bat without any guesswork, do not eat it. It is very easy to mistake a poisonous plant for a perfectly safe one. Definitely do not eat mushrooms unless you are absolutely positive you know which ones they are because some plants have poisons that take days to show symptoms and, by then, it is already too late and it will most likely kill you.

Finally, if you plan on being in an area not for survival purposes and you just want to live off of the land you can often find a local military base where you can ask for a military card for plants in the area or you can buy them online where you can likely get a set of cards. There's also something called "Wild Cards", which will show you edible foods in the form of cards so that you can take it with you and identify edible foods when you're in the wilderness.

Chapter 2 – Easily Identifiable Plants

This section is dedicated to finding the easiest of all the plants, like the onion, and we'll go over how to identify them. Remember that you should look at the real plants themselves in a market or from a store and make sure you can easily identify them before ever trying to eat them in a survival situation. You do not want to be guessing whether the plant you are about to eat will kill you or not.

Onions

Onions are often the easiest to spot in the wilderness and the easiest to identify because they have a signature smell. Just going to the market, purchasing an onion, cutting in half, and then smelling it will give you the sense of smell you need to identify nearly all onions. This teaches you something about what you need to know in order to find edible foods: smell. Most food that you've had on your plate gives off a distinct smell, something that isn't unique to onions but is unique to each plant that has it. Turnips do not have the same smell as onions, which also don't have the same smell as leaks. Smell is the first part of your senses that you can use to easily identify which foods are edible.

Another part of identifying a veggie is sight as in the part of the plant that grows out of the ground. Just go to a farmer's market and memorize what the green part of every plant there looks like. For an onion, the stem is a green shoot that will sometimes curl at the top and there's likely to only be one or two. If I think that I see an onion, I will pull off the stem and smell it to identify what it is. If it smells like an onion then I will dig it out of the ground. Otherwise, I will move on to other veggies. This prevents me from wasting my time and usually ensures I've got a ready to eat veggie because most veggies will only smell a specific way when they are fully matured. The smell comes from the oxidation when the plant releases the oxygen back into the atmosphere for us to breathe.

Chives

This is another veggie that is slightly easy to find since it looks like grass and if you have a bunch of dead leaves around you with just a pocket of what looks like grass, you will automatically think that it is chives. Chives are a hardier plant, unlike grass, and will grow in seemingly inhospitable soil. In order to truly identify what they are, though, you need to pull the roots up and give it a good smell. It will smell like chives bought at the store, which is how you can tell it is not grass. However, an easier way to find them is to look around a creek or some body of water where the area is moist with water as Chives prefer to grow in this area. Therefore, places like rivers or lakes will have Chives not too far off even though you can find them practically anywhere in a wooded environment.

North American Dandelion

This type of Dandelion is very easy to spot due to the unique shape that the leaf has, since it looks like several spearheads on a single stem. Due to this, you will find that they not only are easy to spot but also plentiful in environments that are somewhat moist. We're not talking about the flower itself, which blooms later in the year and is edible on its own or useful for making a wild tea. Instead, we're talking about the leaves, which can be used in a wild salad of different plants. They're relatively low on dietary fiber and the plant grows them to divert bugs away from eating the Dandelion flower. The leaves are easier to get to in comparison to the flower, which stays in a shell until it is ready to bloom and spread its pollen. The root can also be pulled up and baked until it is brown so that you can turn it into a powder for a substitute as coffee.

Cattails or Reeds

This type of plant is commonly found near the bands of rivers where the soil is extremely moist, but it can also be found up further away if the top soil is dry but the underneath is still very moist. Even before the plant is fully mature, you can pull the root of the plant up and peel off the outer coating of the root to get access to the white edible root inside and the white edible stalk of the plant, which will tast similar to that of celery. The reason why these are referred to as Cattails is because the top of the plant will have a solid hot dog looking thing seemingly spiked by the plant. This makes the plant easy to identify when you need to if the plant has fully matured. However, the younger the plant is the more likely you will have to dig into the root in order to get to the edible section of the plant. Now, another useful part about this plant is that you can take the rest of the plant that was part of the root you pulled off and you can boil it. The water you boil it in will be a mild form of mosquito repellent, which can be useful in swampy areas or hot humid months.

Purple Clover

This plant is almost entirely edible and can be used as a salad, but the way you identify it is in its name. The flower is a redish purple and the leaves, themselves, have a chicken foot-like marking on them. These plants are really easy to identify once you know what they look like and they can both serve as food and as tea. There is a thistle that looks like this plant, but to tell them apart there is a green ball underneath the flower and it won't have the mark on the leaves. However, since we cover how you can eat thistles in the Poisonously Edible Plants section, that plant is also edible. This plant is one of those plants that are hard to make a mistake with.

Shamrocks or Wood Sorrel

Shamrocks look like clovers, but the key difference is that clovers have a distinct pattern on their leaves. Shamrocks are edible and they can grow to generally larger sizes given enough time. Most forms of clover are also edible.

Wild Carrots

There are several parts used to identify a wild carrot, of which the first would be that there is an umbel of white flowers and a purple-ish flower in the center of that umbel. Underneath the white flower is a pitchfork like structure that makes a "plant basket" and the steam is covered in fur, but all of it, except the white flower, is green. If you pull this out of the ground, there will be a tumor that smells like a carrot as the root of the plant and the bigger the identified stem the bigger the carrot is going to be. This plant can be confused with water hemlock or just hemlock so be sure that you know the differences before you try and pull this plant. Hemlock's stem will be hairless and have purple blotches, which is the easiest way to identify the difference between the two plants. Hemlock's root also smells like piss.

Orange Daylily

This is a type of flower that is partially edible, as in you can't eat the stem or the core of the flower. The petals are edible and if you dig the root up, there will be an edible white tumor that you can eat attached to the root. This can be confused with the Tiger Lily, which has stripes on its petals.

Curly Dock

You can identify these by the flowers, which will be green with a white center and practically all over the plant. The leaves themselves will be curly, which is where it gets its name. All of the plant is edible and it is really good for those who are low in iron as the plant is full of it. However, if you want a real treat then you should go after the young leaves on this plant as they give off a tart flavor much like candy tarts would. This is not to be confused with Burdock, which will act as a laxative if you eat too much of it but is also edible.

Violet

This is a common flower that you can actually find inside of many backyards, which should making it easier to identify. They are violet, like their name, with a white center and have heart-shaped leaves and they are completely edible.

Garlic Mustard

Another edible plant that grows really quickly, this plant is easily identified through its four-petal white flowers around a seedy center and with leaves that are jagged. Like the name suggests, the plant tastes similar to that of garlic.

Chapter 3 – Poisonously Edible Plants

North American Thistles

Thistles are another type of veggie that are easily identifiable as the end of every leaf will have a prong and the edges will look like it is covered in a white fur. You need to be careful of the fur as this is a poisonous type of plant and the "fur" is really a group of poisonous injectors, which is why it will give a stinging sensation when you try to touch the plant. The poison is called Formic Acid and to get rid of this type of poison all you have to do is boil the toxin out of it, so just sticking it in a boiling pot for a while and letting it boil for a while will gid rid of the toxin. The toxin is detroyed by boiling so the water will also be safe after you have boiled the plant. A fully matured thistle will have a purple flower on the end of its stalks and these plants are edible for most of its life cycle provided that you boil it.

North American Nettles

Another type of plant that has the same Formic Acid as Thistles are Nettles, which tend to grow in the same type of area as the Thistle plant. Unlike the Thistle plant though, it will not grow flowers when it fully matures and will remain a leafy plant all year round. The edible nettle is identified by having leaves that go four different ways, two big side leaves, smaller top and bottom leaves, and then two small leaves in the middle following the same direction as the big side leaves. You can also boil these up and use them in a stew to get a healthy broth for cooking meat and changing the flavor of smaller animals that might not have a friendly taste. If you see a nettle that grows "fruit" stay away from it as it is truly poisonous.

Blackberries

Blackberries are one of the safest berries you can grab to eat and they're easily identifiable due to the fact that they will be black when they are ready to eat. The reason why this is in this section is because you can confuse it with another type of plant called Pokeweed berries. These berries will be dark purple and flat on the outside, kind of like grapes. It only takes a little more than a handful to kill you with Pokeweed, but you can eat blackberries all day long. Likewise, they can be confused with Nightshade, another flat black berry that is actually a notorious poison used in many plot points throughout history.

Wild Cherries

Who doesn't love a good cherry? People who don't like dying from Cyanide poisoning, that's who. If you find wild cherries, be sure to remove the pits of them before trying to put them in your mouth and definitely don't try to do anything else with the plant either as everything but the juice fruits liquid is full of Cyanide.

Milkweed

Milkweeds are very poisonous but their poison can be boiled out provided you have identified the plant correctly and this only applies to their immature fruit. Milkweeds are identified by having the fruit at the top of the plant and the leaves of a Milkweed plant are oval in shape, very big, and have a long yellow spine going down the middle of them. You want to boil the immature fruit twice, once to get the toxin out and then another in separate water to clean them of any remaining toxin.

Acorns

Yes, these are a poisonous type of nut, but only if eaten raw. Like many of the plants in this section, provided you boil the acorns you will find that these little nuts are edible and practically everywhere in the Northern parts of the world. If you don't know what an acorn looks like, it has a round underbelly with a crown of wood on the top of it. Again, if you cannot easily identify a plant then just leave it alone and move on to something you can identify.

Chapter 4 – Medicinal Plants

Broadleaf Plantain

This type of plant is a little difficult to spot in certain cases, but it is the most commonly found medicinal plant in the world because it's really good at growing in harsh soil while also stay close to the ground. The leaves will be a solid green with only a few lines running down the middle of it while also being a nice oval of a leaf and a purple root attaching to the center. Additionally, it will have an enormous shoot growing out of the center, which will have seeds inside of it and those seeds are edible too. Another way to identify them is that they look like a salad bowl with five leaves per layer growing out in a circle. The plant is bitter, which gets better by boiling it, but the plant is better used as an antibiotic than it is a food even though it is edible.

Weeping Willow Bark

There's several different types of Weeping Willow trees, but to identify the tree that is a medicinal plant you need to look at the leaves. The leaf will have a yellowish middle line running from the top to the bottom along with a stem that is also yellowish green. It will be serrated on the edges and will have a spear-like shape. You can boil the bark of the tree and then you have a mild aspirin. Now, most of them will have this same property but the variety of tree determines the strength it will be.

Pine Tree Leaves

The leaves on this type of tree are very thin, like needles (haha it's a pun). Anyway, this is another plant that's good for your immune system rather than just eating it and you can make a lemon-tasting tea out of it that will have some Vitamin C for you. You want to boil the water and then add the pine needles into the tea rather than boiling the pine needles by bring it to a boil with the pine needles in it as bringing it to a boil removes the vitamins you're trying to get from it. These can be confused with Spruce Trees, but Pine Trees are green while Spruce Trees are bluish and produce pinecones.

Red Sumac

Not White Sumac, which will make you itch, but Red Sumac is another type of tree plant that provides a good Vitamin C tea when you boil it. Other than the fact that White Sumac will make you itch upon touch, you can tell if it is a White Sumac if it is covered in red along the leaves and stem of the plant. The plan is identifiable by literally looking for a red cone at the top of the plan, which will be a collection of edible berries. You can either eat it or make a tea out of it, but Red Sumac is edible. When you make a tea out of it, it will actually tastes like lemonade, which is why it is often referred to as Indian Lemonade.

Mayapple

This is another plant that's good for treating diseases like Jaundice. This plant also gives fruit during early springtime. Identifying this plant is relatively easy since it's known as the "umbrella plant". The mature version of this plant will have umbrella-like leaves that are attached with a Y stem with the leaves being, sometimes, nearly a foot wide. Additionally, the flower, if it is there, will be white and will smell very nasty, which is how it protects itself from insects.

GoldenRod

This is another one you can apply to the skin if you grind up the root of the plant so that you can use it as a paste. The identifiable markers on this plant is that the top of the plant will be cover in small yellow flowers, the leaves will be rough to the touch, and the stem will be very long. Only the top will have small yellow flowers. Even though you can make a tea out of this, the entire plant is edible but it is included into this section as you can treat burns you get with the paste made from this plant.

JewelWeed

It is edible after you boil most of it, but, again, it's here because it's better as a medicine. This plant is easily identifiable and you will often find it next to some cattails since the two plants love to grow in similar areas. It's called a JewelWeed because of the shiny red spots that ground on the top of the flower and the fact that it is small enough to be a jewel. The medicinal use is that you can rub it on a rash or a burn to lightly alleviate some of the itching feeling you get from having such an ailment.

The Boneset Plant

The stem is hairy, like unnaturally hairy, and the flowers have clusters of spikes in between them. The leaves of the boneset plant will go around the plant's stem where there will be a single fold running through the middle of the leaf on both sides of the stem, which is a rare trait among plants. These leaves themselves will feel like leather. This is a medicinal plant that was commonly used before we even had an official pharmacy category of medicines to treat all types of fevers caused by infections, which means this plant very useful if you get gangrene.

Conclusion

Welcome to the end of this, but I want to leave off with an important message. Do not one hundred percent rely on this book for all of your information as this is not information you want to mess around with. As shown in the Poisonously Edible Plants section, some of these plants can kill you if you mistake them for other plants or use parts of the plants that are poisonous. Before you touch a plant, you need to make absolutely sure you know what it is and whether it is poisonous or not. With that said, good luck and better surviving.

FREE Bonus Reminder

If you have not grabbed it yet, please go ahead and download your special bonus report *"DIY Projects. 13 Useful & Easy To Make DIY Projects To Save Money & Improve Your Home!"*
Simply Click the Button Below

OR **Go to This Page**
http://diyhomecraft.com/free

BONUS #2: More Free & Discounted Books or Products
Do you want to receive more Free/Discounted Books or Products?
We have a mailing list where we send out our new Books or Products when they go free or with a discount on Amazon. Click on the link below to sign up for Free & Discount Book & Product Promotions.
=> Sign Up for Free & Discount Book & Product Promotions <=

OR Go to this URL
http://zbit.ly/1WBb1Ek

Printed in Great Britain
by Amazon